IT'S OUTTA HERE!

THE MIGHT AND MAJESTY OF THE HOME RUN

MATT DOEDEN

MILLBROOK PRESS · MINNEAPOLIS

**For Dad and the endless hours
he played catch and pitched to me**

Millbrook Press™
An imprint of Lerner Publishing Group, Inc.
241 First Avenue North
Minneapolis, MN 55401 USA

For reading levels and more information, look up this title at www.lernerbooks.com.

Designed by Mary Ross & Sue Feinhage

Main body text set in Adobe Garamond Pro.
Typeface provided by Adobe Systems.

Library of Congress Cataloging-in-Publication Data

Names: Doeden, Matt, author.
Title: It's outta here! : the might and majesty of the home run / Matt Doeden.
Description: Minneapolis : Millbrook Press, 2021. | Series: Spectacular sports
  | Includes bibliographical references and index. | Audience: Ages 10–18
  | Audience: Grades 4–6 | Summary: "For more than one hundred years,
  the home run has been the most exciting play in baseball. Read about the
  longest, strangest, and most important home runs in Major League Baseball
  history"— Provided by publisher.
Identifiers: LCCN 2020020855 (print) | LCCN 2020020856 (ebook) | ISBN
  9781728417165 (library binding) | ISBN 9781728419084 (ebook)
Subjects: LCSH: Home runs (Baseball)—Juvenile literatue. | Baseball—United
  States—History—Juvenile literature.
Classification: LCC GV868.4 .D64 2021 (print) | LCC GV868.4 (ebook) | DDC
  796.357/26—dc23

LC record available at https://lccn.loc.gov/2020020855
LC ebook record available at https://lccn.loc.gov/2020020856

Manufactured in the United States of America
1-48970-49230-10/26/2020

CONTENTS

INTRODUCTION
GOING DEEP

The pitcher looks in to the catcher for the sign and delivers. It's a fastball, high in the strike zone, and the batter is ready. Within a fraction of a second, the hitter figures out the pitch's spin and location and begins to swing. *Crack!* The ball launches off the bat at more than 100 miles (161 km) per hour. It sails down the left-field line.

The crowd roars as the left fielder sprints toward the corner. Will the ball be fair or foul? Will it have enough distance to clear the fence? It soars just inside the foul pole. Home run! It's the biggest play in baseball, and nothing gets fans more excited.

Mike Trout of the Los Angeles
Angels hits a home run in 2019.
Trout hit 302 homers in his first ten
Major League Baseball seasons.

In 2019 Miguel Sanó was one of five Minnesota Twins players to hit at least 30 home runs.

1 THE LONG HISTORY OF THE LONG BALL

With home runs flying out of ballparks at a record pace, baseball had never seen anything like the 2019 season. Baseball's modern era, stretching nearly 120 years, has seen its highs and lows. It has witnessed power surges and power outages. But 2019 was special: it was the year of the home run.

From opening day, it was clear that 2019 would be a standout season. The standing record for team home runs in a season was 267. Four teams overtook that mark in 2019. The Minnesota Twins broke the record on August 31—with a full month to go in the season. And the Twins kept slugging. They didn't just break the home run record. They destroyed it. Minnesota went on to set a new record with 307 home runs, and they did it in a home ballpark long considered pitcher-friendly. The New York Yankees were close behind, slugging 306 big flies. Individual records fell by the wayside as well. New York Mets first baseman Pete Alonso hit 53 long balls, the most ever by a rookie.

Major League Baseball (MLB) struggled to explain the remarkable season. Had something changed with the materials that made up the balls? Were the hitters that much better, or had they made changes to their swings that helped them hit long blasts? But the biggest question focused on baseball's future. In a sport where fans loved the home run, did MLB want the long-ball trend to continue?

THE REIGN AND FALL OF THE DEAD BALL

Baseball wasn't always centered on hitting the ball over the fence. In the early 1900s, MLB games were built around a strategy that modern fans call small ball. Players didn't swing for the fences. They tried to get on base. They bunted and focused on making contact with the ball. The game was about methodically moving runners from base to base, not bringing them all home with one swing of the bat.

During the dead ball era, from 1900 to 1919, the home run was a novelty, an afterthought. In both 1905 and 1909, not a single MLB player reached double digits in home runs. Baseball historians have several theories about why the home run was such a rarity for the first two decades of the century. During that time, MLB allowed pitchers to throw spitballs. Pitchers doctored balls with sticky substances to affect their flight, possibly leading to low home run totals. The spitball was banned in 1920 and home run totals surged. Others point to changes in ballpark sizes, pitching strategies, or how baseballs were manufactured. Probably all of these contributed to the low home run totals.

Historians agree, however, about the player who was most responsible for ending the dead ball era. It was a young pitcher-turned-slugger who went on to rewrite baseball's record books. It was Babe Ruth.

During the dead ball era, many hitters choked up on the bat to help make contact with the ball, reducing the power of their swings.

RUTH USHERS IN A NEW AGE

Babe Ruth played his first MLB game in 1914 with the Boston Red Sox. He spent the first four seasons of his career almost exclusively as a pitcher—and he was a good one. In 1916 he went 23–12 and led the American League (AL) with an earned run average (ERA) of 1.75. He was the hero of the 1918 World Series, winning both of his starts and allowing just two runs in 17 innings.

Ruth could have continued his brilliant career as a starting pitcher. But in 1918, he convinced Red Sox manager Ed Barrow to let him play in the field on days Ruth didn't pitch. It proved to be a game-changing decision. Ruth slugged a league-leading 11 home runs in 1918. The 1919 season started out the same, with Ruth as a pitcher first and a hitter second. But as he cranked out

Babe Ruth throws a pitch for the Red Sox.

home runs at a pace the game had never before seen, the Red Sox began to use him mainly as a hitter. Barrow saw that Ruth could change the game at the plate. And that's exactly what Ruth did. He hit an almost unthinkable 29 home runs that year, shattering the MLB record.

Ruth's power surge in 1919 marked a shift in how the game was played. Home runs were no longer an afterthought. Ruth was on a path to become the biggest star the game had ever seen.

Babe Ruth watches his 60th home run of the season soar out of Yankee Stadium on September 30, 1927.

After the 1919 season, the Red Sox sold Ruth's contract to the New York Yankees. Ruth donned the Yankees pinstripes, an event that many historians call the beginning of baseball's golden age (1920–1960). In 1920 Ruth hit 54 home runs. That was almost five times more than he'd hit in 1918 to win the AL home run title. In 1921 he raised the bar again, slugging 59 home runs. Six seasons later, he blasted 60 dingers, a record that stood for almost 35 years. As Ruth set records, the rest of baseball was catching up. In 1921 just six batters hit 20 or more dingers. In 1930, 19 batters did it.

The game had evolved. The dead ball era was over, and the defining feature of the golden age was the home run.

INTEGRATION AND A NEW WAVE OF SLUGGERS

On the field, baseball advanced by leaps and bounds in the 1920s and 1930s. The game finally resembled the version that modern fans know. It was more popular than ever. MLB was spreading across the country, growing its fan base and expanding into new markets.

Yet socially, the game reflected the racist beliefs of many white people in this era. By unwritten agreement, MLB owners did not employ people of color as players. People of color who wanted to play pro baseball joined the Negro Leagues, a group of loosely organized teams. Negro Leagues players earned just a fraction of the money their MLB counterparts earned, and games lacked the media coverage and fanfare of the big leagues.

World War II (1939–1945) played a role in opening MLB to everyone. US soldiers of all colors fought and died together in Europe and in the Pacific theater. In Europe the United States battled Nazi Germany. Led by dictator Adolf Hitler, the Nazis preached German racial superiority and killed people of other ethnic backgrounds—especially Jewish people—by the millions. When the United States and its allies won the war in 1945, many soldiers, including some baseball players, came back with new views on race relations. If soldiers of different races could share a battlefield, why couldn't they share a baseball field?

Branch Rickey was general manager of the Brooklyn Dodgers. He was ready to change the game. In October 1945, Rickey signed Jackie Robinson, an infielder in the Negro Leagues, to a contract. In 1946 Robinson played for the Montreal Royals, then a minor-league team of the Dodgers. On April 15, 1947, he finally took the field for the Dodgers, breaking baseball's color barrier. Three days later,

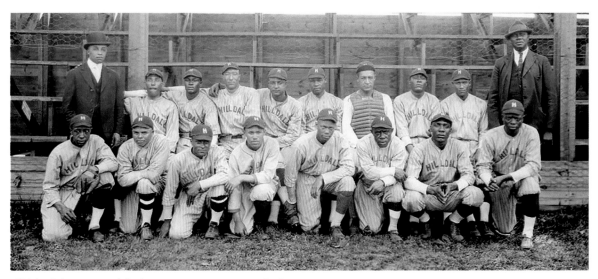

Hilldale Club was one of the best Negro Leagues teams in the 1920s.

JOSH GIBSON

Babe Ruth was the greatest home run hitter of his era. He didn't have much competition in the major leagues for the title. But one man—Negro Leagues star Josh Gibson—could have been just as good.

Gibson was pure power. The Negro Leagues didn't keep stats for all their games, so no one knows exactly how many dingers Gibson hit. But some experts say it could be more than 800. Gibson blasted mammoth shots. One of his home runs soared 580 feet (177 m). According to a fellow player, Gibson once hit a ball completely out of Yankee Stadium, over the third deck in left field. That's a feat Ruth never accomplished.

Gibson's home runs made him a legend, but his life was marred by tragedy. In 1930 his wife, Helen, died during childbirth. In 1943 Gibson fell ill with a brain tumor. He never fully recovered. Despite crippling headaches, Gibson returned to baseball. He died of a stroke on January 20, 1947—just three months before Jackie Robinson's debut with the Dodgers. Gibson was 35 years old. He was elected to the National Baseball Hall of Fame in 1972.

Robinson belted his first major-league home run, a line drive to left field in the third inning against the New York Giants.

Robinson became an excellent player for the Dodgers and helped Brooklyn win the 1955 World Series. His debut also opened the door for a new wave of sluggers. More players of color began to join MLB, including legends such as Willie Mays and Hank Aaron.

Jackie Robinson hit 137 career home runs for the Dodgers.

MARIS CHASES DOWN RUTH

The 1961 season was remarkable for fans of home runs. Two Yankees—Mickey Mantle and Roger Maris—belted home runs at a record pace. To many baseball fans, it was no surprise to see Mantle make a run at Ruth's 1927 long-ball record. Mantle was a rising star, had a bright future, and was beloved by fans.

Maris was quiet and shy. He didn't like the media attention that grew as the season wore on and he drew ever closer to the 60-homer record. Yet when an infection slowed Mantle's home run pace, Maris bore the full attention of the baseball world—including many fans who hoped he wouldn't catch the legendary Ruth.

Maris, despite being visibly worn down by the stress of the pursuit, hit his 60th home run on September 26. Four games remained on the schedule—four opportunities to break Ruth's record. Three of them came and went without the record-breaking blast.

Roger Maris hit his 45th homer of the season in the second game of a doubleheader on August 14, 1961.

In the final game of the season, the Yankees hosted the Red Sox. Maris stepped to the plate in the bottom of the fourth inning of a scoreless game. So many New York fans didn't want to see Maris pass Ruth that the stadium stood half empty. Boston pitcher Tracy Stallard delivered a pitch, and Maris took a big cut. He launched a line drive to deep right field. It cleared the fence, and Maris circled the bases as baseball's new single-season home run champion.

A remarkable achievement, but some argued that the record was tainted. Ruth hit 60 home runs when baseball had a 154-game schedule, while Maris played a 162-game schedule in 1961. Baseball's commissioner at the time even declared that Maris's total should be marked with an asterisk in record books, since he'd played in more games.

Maris never got over the cold treatment he received from fans. "They acted as though I was doing something wrong, poisoning the record books or something," he said. In the years to come, Maris couldn't duplicate his amazing home run output of 1961, but his record-breaking season secured his place among the game's greatest sluggers.

THE SECOND DEAD BALL ERA

Maris's record-setting season came near the end of baseball's golden age. The era of the home run was ending. In 1961 MLB teams averaged 0.95 home runs per game. That mark was on par with the peak of the golden age, when home run rates hovered around 0.90. But during the rest of the 1960s, that rate dropped dramatically. Power-armed

Roger Maris (*left*) poses with teammates Yogi Berra (*middle*) and Mickey Mantle on the dugout steps in 1961.

pitchers such as Sandy Koufax and Bob Gibson ushered in an era of lower-scoring baseball—with a lot fewer home runs. By 1968 the home run rate had dropped to 0.61 long balls per game.

That didn't mean the game was without its sluggers. In 1974 Hank Aaron hit his 715th long ball to pass Ruth as MLB's career home run king. Harmon Killebrew, Frank Robinson, and Reggie Jackson electrified fans with moon shots. But on the whole, players were hitting home runs at the lowest rates since the dead ball era.

The reasons for the drop aren't entirely clear. It may have been better pitching. Or it could have been changes in how baseballs were manufactured—including a change in 1974 from horsehide to cowhide covers.

Sandy Koufax won three Cy Young Awards as the National League's best pitcher and helped the Los Angeles Dodgers win three World Series.

SADAHARU OH

North America isn't the only hotbed for baseball. The sport is popular around the world, and it's especially huge in Japan. The country has its own home run king: Sadaharu Oh. Oh was born in Tokyo, Japan, on May 20, 1940. Like Babe Ruth, he started his professional career as a pitcher. But Oh made history as a hitter. Oh used his trademark flamingo leg kick to help generate amazing power at the plate. From 1959 to 1980, Oh belted 868 home runs. He went on to a successful career as a manager, leading Japan to a championship in the first World Baseball Classic in 2006.

Whatever the reasons, home run rates remained low for nearly three decades. It's a period that some have termed baseball's second dead ball era. Then, in the mid-1990s, things suddenly changed in some very big ways.

MCGWIRE AND SOSA TAKE FLIGHT

Mark McGwire clubs his 62nd home run of the season to break Roger Maris's record.

Starting in 1994, Major League Baseball experienced a home run surge unlike any since Ruth changed the game in 1920. Throughout the 1980s and early 1990s, home run rates hovered around 0.80 per game. Then, in 1994, they suddenly jumped to 1.03—and kept rising.

At first, it was hard to explain. Almost overnight, big leaguers were hitting home runs at rates fans had never seen. Suddenly, no home run records were safe. In 1998 two players—Mark McGwire of the St. Louis Cardinals and Sammy Sosa of the Chicago Cubs—launched an assault on Maris's single-season record that ignited fan interest as never before.

For many people, it was riveting baseball. Big Mac and Slammin' Sammy traded monster home runs almost nightly. By the beginning of September, both men stood at 55 home runs, just seven away from breaking Maris's record.

The countdowns were on, and it didn't take long. McGwire got hot in the first week of September, pulling ahead of Sosa and tying Maris on September 7—the first date of a two-game series against Sosa's Cubs.

On September 8, the eyes of the baseball world were on St. Louis. MLB issued special baseballs with invisible marks to use every time McGwire stepped to the plate. If he hit a homer, officials could use the mark on the ball to prove it was the genuine record-breaker. Big Mac grounded out in his first at bat. He stepped to the plate in the bottom of the fourth with another shot at history. McGwire swung at the first pitch he saw from Chicago pitcher Steve Trachsel. It wasn't one of his trademark moon shots, but McGwire got just enough of it. The low line drive sailed over the left-field fence as the stadium erupted. Sosa applauded and fireworks boomed as McGwire circled the bases.

The joyful scene was far different from the one Maris experienced in 1961 when he broke Ruth's record. McGwire and Sosa's remarkable chase went on. McGwire finished the 1998 season with 70 home runs, while Sosa had 66. They left no doubt that a new live ball era was underway.

TAINTED RECORDS

Most fans and reporters embraced the home run chase of 1998. Yet even at the time, people had questions. Why were some hitters suddenly blasting home runs at an increased pace? Was it pure skill? Did the baseballs change so they'd fly farther? Or was it something else?

In 2001 Barry Bonds of the San Francisco Giants launched his own assault on the record books. It was the finest hitting performance in the history of baseball. Bonds was so lethal at the plate that many pitchers didn't even try to get him out and intentionally walked him instead. Bonds took 177 walks that year. Since walks don't count as official at bats, he had just 476 at bats all season. Yet he hammered 73 home runs—one for every 6.5 official trips to the plate. The numbers were almost unthinkable. The incredible performance seemed too good to be true.

And as it happened, it probably was. Around this time, it was becoming clear that many of the game's top players used performance-enhancing drugs (PEDs) such as anabolic steroids to artificially boost their muscles. Three of the players named in the scandal were McGwire, Sosa, and Bonds—along with many others.

STEROIDS

PEDs were one of MLB's biggest story lines in the late 1990s and early 2000s. The period is often called the steroids era. PEDs include a wide range of substances designed to improve performance and speed up recovery from injuries. During the steroids era, the majority of documented cases of PED use in baseball involved anabolic steroids.

Most anabolic steroids are created in a lab. In the human body, the substances act similarly to testosterone, a natural hormone that contributes to muscle growth. In the 1990s and 2000s, some MLB players used anabolic steroids to grow stronger, hit the ball farther, and recover from injuries more quickly.

Using steroids comes with serious medical risks. They can contribute to medical problems from liver failure to heart disease. Steroids also create an unfair advantage for athletes who use them. MLB officially banned steroids in 1991 but did not actively test players for them until 2003.

The steroids accusations left many fans bitter. Bonds broke Hank Aaron's career home run record in 2007. The feat should have come with incredible fanfare. Yet by then, fans and the media widely believed that Bonds had used PEDs for at least part of his career. Fans treated his stats with a mix of disinterest and hostility. Instead of being hailed as a baseball hero, they widely regarded Bonds as a villain. Records that fans once held dear seemed tainted. The home run had lost some of its luster.

Yet even after the league began widespread steroid testing in 2003, the home runs kept coming. One reason may have been a wave of new hitter-friendly ballparks with outfield fences placed relatively close to home plate. Home run rates remained high, then spiked like never before in 2019 with an average of 1.39 home runs per game. It was by far the most home runs ever hit, and MLB officials said they didn't understand why. Did 2019 mark the beginning of a new ultra-live ball era? Or was the long ball assault a blip on the radar that would fade away as quickly as it emerged?

2 THE PHYSICS OF THE HOME RUN

What does it take to hit a home run? It's not as simple as swinging hard. How far a baseball soars is affected by everything from bat speed and launch angle to ballpark size and climate conditions. Read on to learn more about the physics of the home run.

THE PITCH

A home run doesn't begin with the batter's swing. It starts the moment the pitcher releases the ball. The pitch must be in or near the strike zone to give the batter a reasonable chance of making good contact. Most home runs come on pitches that are in the top half of the strike zone. These pitches are easier to drive in the air because they allow for swings at the right angle to send the ball soaring.

Even the type of pitch can have an impact on home runs. Fastballs are blasted over outfield fences at higher rates than other pitches. Fastballs travel with great velocity and often cross the plate high in the strike zone—both of which lead to a lot of hard-hit fly balls. The movement and lower velocities of curveballs, changeups, and other pitches make them harder to hit with the fat part of the bat.

THE SWING

Once the pitch is released, baseball becomes a game of milliseconds. A 90-mile-per-hour (145 km) fastball reaches home plate in 400 milliseconds, or 0.4 seconds. But a batter has about half that much time to decide to swing the bat. Within 200 to 250 milliseconds, the hitter must identify the pitch's location and spin and begin to swing.

Any home run requires solid contact. Batters try to hit the ball with the sweet spot of the bat, the fat part of the barrel as close to dead center as possible. This way they can transfer the most energy from the bat to the ball.

Once the bat makes contact with the ball, several factors determine how far it will fly. The first two are related—the weight and speed of the bat. The heavier the

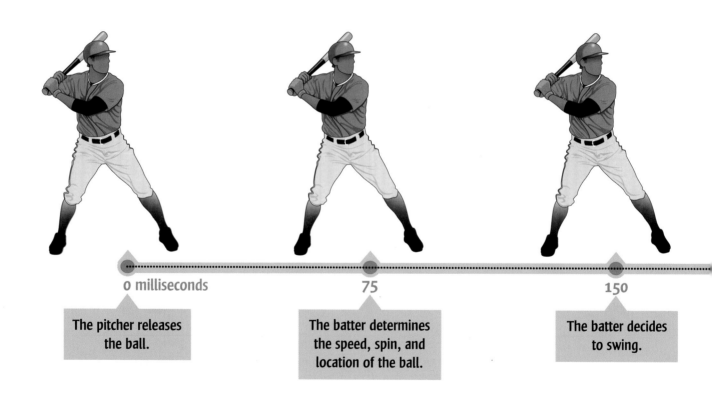

0 milliseconds

The pitcher releases the ball.

75

The batter determines the speed, spin, and location of the ball.

150

The batter decides to swing.

bat and the faster it travels through the strike zone, the more kinetic energy—the energy of movement—it carries. The most powerful hitters can reach bat speeds of more than 100 miles (161 km) per hour.

The speed of the pitch, the speed and weight of the bat, and the ability of the batter to hit the sweet spot work together to transfer kinetic energy to the ball. The speed at which the ball leaves the bat is called its exit velocity. Most home runs require an exit velocity above 100 miles (161 km) per hour to clear the fences. Truly mammoth home runs can have exit velocities of more than 120 miles (193 km) per hour.

When it comes to hitting home runs, exit velocity is only part of the story. Another factor is launch angle, the angle at which the ball leaves the bat. If the

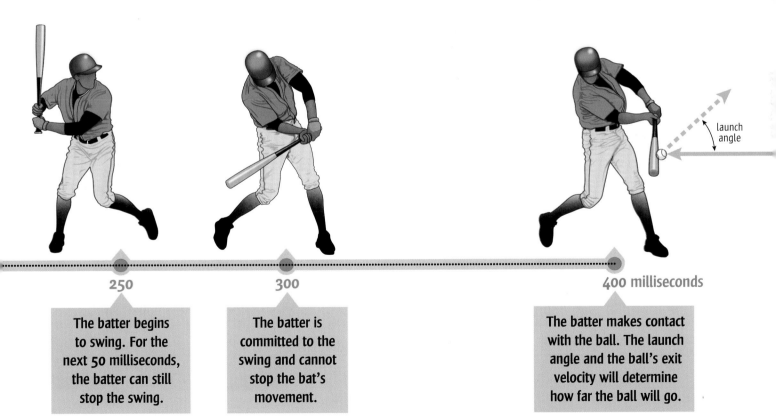

launch angle

250

The batter begins to swing. For the next 50 milliseconds, the batter can still stop the swing.

300

The batter is committed to the swing and cannot stop the bat's movement.

400 milliseconds

The batter makes contact with the ball. The launch angle and the ball's exit velocity will determine how far the ball will go.

When an MLB player hits the ball on the sweet spot of the bat and produces the right launch angle, the ball often lands in the outfield stands a few seconds later.

launch angle is down, the swing will drive the ball into the ground. A launch angle that is flat or nearly flat will be a line drive that usually doesn't soar far enough or high enough to clear the outfield fence. When the launch angle is too high, the result is a high fly ball or a pop-up. All of that kinetic energy is spent sending the ball up instead of up and out.

To hit one over the outfield fence, a hitter needs a launch angle of around 15 to 35 degrees, with 25 to 30 degrees being ideal. This angle gives the ball enough height and the powerful outward push it needs to clear the fence.

GAME CONDITIONS

The physics of the home run don't end with the swing. For a 500-foot (152 m) blast, the ballpark conditions probably won't matter. The ball is going out no matter how tall the outfield fence is or which way the wind is blowing. But usually the ballpark and the game conditions play big roles in whether a ball goes out or lands safely in an outfielder's glove.

In the National Basketball Association and the National Football League, the courts and fields are always the same size. But MLB fields are different. Some parks, such as Yankee Stadium, are havens for hitters because

Yankee Stadium

BIG BLAST STATS

What makes a big home run? Check out the vital statistics on 2019's longest blasts!

Date	Batter	Exit velocity miles (km)/hour	Launch angle	Distance traveled feet (m)
June 21	Nomar Mazara	109.7 (176.5)	27.2	505 (154)
September 12	Rangel Ravelo	111.5 (179.4)	26.3	487 (148)
June 10	Ian Desmond	110.8 (178.3)	27.9	486 (148)
March 28	Nomar Mazara	112.1 (180.4)	25.3	482 (147)
June 2	Ketel Marte	111.9 (180.1)	23.0	482 (147)
June 21	Gary Sanchez	113.4 (182.5)	23.5	481 (147)
June 27	Ryan McMahon	108.3 (174.3)	28.6	479 (146)
August 27	Jackie Bradley Jr.	112.1 (180.4)	29.6	478 (146)
June 2	Chris Iannetta	113.1 (182)	33.3	476 (145)
April 7	Josh Bell	113.3 (182.3)	21.8	474 (144)
August 5	Ian Happ	108.6 (174.8)	32.2	474 (144)
August 10	Carlos Correa	111.6 (179.6)	28.2	474 (144)

the outfield fences are relatively close to home plate. Boston's Fenway Park has a center-field fence that is just 390 feet (119 m) away. Others are much farther. The center-field fence in Houston's Minute Maid Park measures 436 feet (133 m) from home.

The fences in left field and right field may be even more important, since that's where the majority of home runs go. In Fenway Park, the right-field fence is 302 feet (92 m) from home plate, while Chicago's Wrigley Field has a right-field fence a whopping 353 feet (108 m) away. And distance is just part of the equation. Some outfield fences are short enough to allow outfielders to leap up and snatch would-be

A home run lands in the grass just beyond the reach of St. Louis Cardinals center fielder Harrison Bader.

home runs. Others are much taller—and harder to clear. Not all ballparks are created equally, and they play major roles in home run rates.

Weather also has a big impact on how far a ball will travel. The biggest weather factors are wind and air density. Wind blowing in toward home plate from the outfield will shorten the flight of a batted ball hit in that direction. Wind blowing out will help a ball carry. A breeze of just 5 miles (8 km) per hour can help a ball soar as much as 19 feet (6 m) farther than it would on its own. The stronger the wind, the bigger the boost.

"When the wind is blowing in, you really try to keep the ball out of the air as much as you can, and try to hit the ball on a line drive that can get through the wind," said Hall-of-Fame outfielder Rickey Henderson. "Sometimes, when the wind is blowing in and you hit a high fly ball you feel is out of the ballpark, the wind will hold it up and it's just a deep [out]."

Air density is a bit more complex. It's influenced by a range of factors, including temperature, atmospheric pressure, humidity, and elevation. Air slows down the ball as it flies. The ball pushes against molecules of air—and they push back. So the denser and heavier the air, the more it will slow down the ball.

Home runs are easiest to hit in places with low air density. High temperature, high humidity, low atmospheric pressure, and high elevation all help to reduce air density. It's easier to hit a home run on a day that's 90°F (32°C) and humid than 50°F (10°C) and dry. That's because warm, wet air is less dense and baseballs meet less resistance as they fly toward the outfield seats.

TAMING COORS FIELD

When MLB expanded to Denver, Colorado, in 1993, unexpected consequences occurred. The Colorado Rockies played their first two seasons in Mile High Stadium before moving into a new ballpark, Coors Field (*below*), in 1995.

Coors Field stands in the Rocky Mountains, 5,200 feet (1,585 m) above sea level. That's almost five times the elevation of any other big-league park. The stadium's designers understood that air density drops with elevation, and they knew that meant the ball would carry well at Coors. They tried to compensate by adding deep outfield fences. But it wasn't enough. Coors Field immediately became a home run hitter's paradise. Balls flew out of the stadium at a record pace.

In 2002 the Rockies added a humidor to Coors Field, a special room where they stored all the game balls. The humidor humidified the balls, giving them a wetter, less springy texture. Home runs at Coors Field dropped. But its high elevation and low air density still make it one of the most home-run-friendly ballparks in the big leagues.

3 HISTORY'S MOST MEMORABLE HOME RUNS

For pure baseball excitement, it's hard to beat a home run. One swing of the bat can change a game, turn a playoff series, or bring home World Series glory. Relive some of the most memorable long balls in major-league history.

RUTH CALLS HIS SHOT
October 1, 1932

No moment in baseball history is more steeped in mystery and legend than the most famous home run of Babe Ruth's amazing career. It came during Game 3 of the 1932 World Series between the Yankees and the Cubs.

It had been a fiery series, with both teams—and their fans—loudly talking trash. According to the legend, Cubs fans went so far as to throw fruit at Ruth during his batting practice before Game 3. Emotions were running high, and Ruth was eager to remind everyone that *he* was baseball's greatest slugger and that they were not. He

Ruth's two blasts in Game 3 helped the Yankees beat the Cubs 7–5. New York crushed Chicago 13–6 in Game 4 to sweep the World Series.

wasted little time in doing just that. In the first inning, Ruth came to the plate with two runners on base and promptly blasted a three-run home run to deep center field.

The Cubs charged back to tie the game 4–4. In the top of the fifth, Ruth strolled to the plate with one out and nobody on base. Chicago pitcher Charlie Root delivered a first-pitch strike, followed by two balls. Ruth fouled off the fourth offering, leaving the count even at two balls, two strikes. And this is where the legend was born.

Ruth stepped out of the batter's box and pointed two fingers toward center field. Was he pointing at the pitcher? Or at the fence beyond? Was he reminding everyone that he had just two strikes against him? Baseball historians don't agree on just what Ruth's gesture was supposed to mean. But no one can argue about what happened next. Ruth took a monumental hack at the 2–2 pitch and drove it nearly to the flagpole beyond the center-field fence.

Sportswriters had a field day with the gesture and the blast, proclaiming that Ruth had called his shot. Was it true? Early on, Ruth dismissed the idea. But later, he claimed he did predict the homer. The debate lives on, and it's unlikely baseball fans will ever agree. But one thing is certain. Ruth's called shot—real or not—stands as the most legendary moment of a legendary career.

THE SHOT HEARD ROUND THE WORLD
October 3, 1951

On August 11, 1951, the race for the National League (NL) title appeared to be all but over. The Brooklyn Dodgers led the New York Giants by a whopping 13 games with a little more than a month to play.

But somehow, it wasn't over. The Giants went 37–7 to end the season, including winning their last seven games, to pull into a tie for first place. That forced a best-of-three series between the Giants and the Dodgers for a trip to the World Series. The teams split the first two games, forcing a deciding Game 3. And what a game it was.

The Dodgers took a 4–1 lead into the ninth inning. Once again, the Giants needed a comeback. After a pair of singles, Whitey Lockman stroked a double, driving in one runner.

Bobby Thomson, who had hit 32 home runs for the Giants during the season, stepped to the plate as the winning run. He faced the hard-throwing Ralph Branca. Thomson connected on Branca's second pitch, sending it deep over the left-field fence. One of the most remarkable comebacks in baseball history was complete, and Thomson's home run—nicknamed the Shot Heard Round the World—became the stuff of legend.

MANTLE'S HUGE BLAST
April 17, 1953

According to many, Babe Ruth holds the record for the longest home run ever hit, a 1919 dinger that may have traveled 587 feet (179 m). The trouble with Ruth's record is that nobody officially measured the home run. Baseball writers of the day agreed on 587 feet, but it was really just an estimate. We can't be sure exactly how far it flew.

For those who prefer hard numbers, the king of all home runs came off the bat of Mickey Mantle on April 17, 1953. It was an ordinary early-season game that would have been forgotten by history if not for one swing of the bat from the 21-year-old Mantle. He came up to bat in the top of the fifth. His Yankees were clinging to a 2–1 lead over the Washington Senators. With catcher Yogi Berra on base, Mantle stepped in.

It was a windy day, and the ball was carrying well at Griffith Stadium in Washington, DC. Left-hander Chuck Stobbs delivered a high fastball, and Mantle pounced. With a great crack of the bat, he drove a long, high drive to left field. With the wind blowing out, the ball just kept sailing. It completely cleared the bleachers and banged high off a sign 460 feet (140 m) from home plate. The ball kept rolling to a distance of 565 feet (172 m).

MICKEY MANTLE'S TITANIC 565-FOOT HOME RUN
HIT RIGHT-HANDED, FIFTH INNING, AGAINST WASHINGTON SENATORS, CHUCK STOBBS PITCHING. GRIFFITH STADIUM, APRIL 17, 1953

This graphic shows the flight path of Mantle's home run.

Yankees coach Bill Dickey had seen some of the greatest home runs in baseball history, but even he was amazed. "I saw Babe and Lou [Gehrig] hit balls out of parks all over the country, also I was catching when fellows like Jimmie Foxx were blasting pitches a good country mile," he said. "Frankly, I never thought I'd see their like again, but now I've changed my mind."

The blast against the Senators was perhaps the most impressive of Mantle's fine career. He went on to hit 536 career home runs, good for 18th on MLB's all-time list. Many baseball experts believe he would rank even higher if leg injuries had not hampered him for much of his career.

MAZ ENDS THE GREATEST GAME
October 13, 1960

Game 7 of the 1960 World Series has been called the Greatest Game Ever Played. Not everyone agrees, but no one denies that it was a thrilling way to end the season. The Pittsburgh Pirates had come into the World Series as huge underdogs to the powerful Yankees. New York's lineup was loaded with the biggest names in baseball, while the Pirates were a group of relative unknowns.

It shouldn't have been close. The Yankees outscored the Pirates 46–17 in the first six games. Yet somehow the series was tied 3–3.

Pittsburgh's hopes looked dim in Game 7. In the bottom of the eighth inning, they trailed 7–4. Then they exploded for five runs to take the lead . . . only to watch New York tie it 9–9 in the top of the ninth.

Bill Mazeroski led off the bottom of the ninth for the Pirates. Maz was an outstanding player—some have called him the best defensive second baseman of all time. But he wasn't much of a hitter. He certainly wouldn't have looked that threatening to Yankees closer Ralph Terry.

Maz later confessed that he was a bit dazed as he stepped to the plate. The New York rally in the top of the ninth had left him rattled. He hadn't even realized at first that he was due to bat. He took the first pitch, a ball. Then came the second pitch. Maz liked what he saw and took a big swing. He connected with a mammoth shot, driving the ball more than 400 feet (122 m) over the high left-field wall.

The Pirates had done it. Maz's walk-off home run completed a huge World Series upset. And it remains the only Game 7 walk-off home run in World Series history.

AARON CHASES DOWN RUTH
April 8, 1974

As the 1973 baseball season drew to a close, all eyes were on Atlanta Braves slugger Hank Aaron. He was closing in on Babe Ruth's career home run record of 714. While many fans were rooting for Aaron and eager to see history, not everyone shared their enthusiasm. Some didn't want Ruth's legendary record to fall to anyone, and certainly not to a Black man.

African Americans and other people of color had faced centuries of oppression in the US. But by the 1970s, thanks to the civil rights movement, racial minorities were beginning to achieve greater equality. Yet even with these gains, racism remained a significant problem, and Aaron's pursuit of Ruth was a lightning rod. Aaron received piles of hate mail. People threatened his

Aaron hit at least 40 home runs in a season eight times.

life. An achievement that should have been the greatest of his career became a nightmare.

Aaron was undoubtedly eager to end the chase quickly and get out of the spotlight. But it didn't work out that way. Aaron went cold at the end of the 1973 season and finished at 713 home runs—one shy of Ruth. He would have to wait until 1974 to resume the chase.

Finally, on April 4, 1974, Aaron belted number 714, pulling even with Ruth on the home run list. The pressure to hit just one more grew.

Four days later, the Braves hosted the Los Angeles Dodgers. Aaron took a walk in his first at bat. In the fourth inning, with the Braves trailing 3–1, he came to the plate with a runner on base. He turned to the on-deck circle, where his teammate Dusty Baker waited to follow Aaron to the plate. "Hey, I'm going to get this over with," Aaron said to Baker. "Right now!"

That's exactly what he did. On the second pitch from Dodgers pitcher Al Downing, Aaron took a healthy cut. He drove a high fastball deep to left-center field. The ball cleared the fence, landing in the bullpen. Home run 715! The wait was finally over, and Aaron was MLB's new all-time home run king. As he circled the bases, two fans ran out onto the field—and straight toward Aaron. With the death threats Aaron had received, seeing two people running onto the field was unnerving for many. But the fans meant no harm. They ran alongside him briefly, offering congratulations before running away. Aaron was free to celebrate with his teammates. The long chase was over.

Aaron went on to belt 755 career home runs. He retired in 1976 as MLB's all-time home run champion, a record that stood until Barry Bonds broke it in 2007. Yet because of allegations of steroid abuse by Bonds, many still think of Hammerin' Hank as baseball's true home run king.

BODY LANGUAGE
October 21, 1975

The 1975 World Series was a barn burner. The tight, back-and-forth series between the Red Sox and Cincinnati Reds had fans on the edges of their seats. Game 6 was the most thrilling of them all.

The powerful Reds led the series 3–2 and wanted to close out the Red Sox. It looked like they would do it, taking a 6–3 lead in the top of the eighth inning. But Boston bounced back in the bottom of the inning to tie it.

The game remained 6–6 in the bottom of the 12th inning. Boston catcher Carlton Fisk stepped up. On the second pitch Fisk saw, he lifted a long fly ball down the left-field line. It had the distance to go over the fence. But would it drift into foul territory? Everyone in Fenway Park tried to will the ball to stay fair—including Fisk. He wildly waved his arms to the right, as if he could push the ball to the fair side of the foul pole.

The ball stayed fair—by inches. Fisk's home run forced Game 7 the next day. In the end, Boston's comeback fell short as Cincinnati won the series. But Fisk's home run remains one of the most iconic moments in baseball history.

Fisk waves his arms as his game-winning homer soars toward the left-field foul pole.

MR. OCTOBER IS BORN
October 18, 1977

For most teams, 15 years without a World Series title is no big deal. But for Yankees fans in 1977, it felt like an eternity. Since the 1920s, the New York fan base had

Reggie Jackson sees three pitches and hits three home runs in Game 6 of the 1977 World Series.

lived through more than four decades of MLB dominance, and they weren't used to waiting so long between titles.

Before the season, slugger Reggie Jackson joined the Yankees. His five-year contract, worth about $3 million, was massive for the time. And not everyone was convinced he deserved that much money. Among Jackson's biggest critics was his own manager, Billy Martin. Jackson had a good first season in New York. He slugged 32 home runs and drove in 110 runs, but his performance still wasn't enough for some.

During the World Series Jackson quieted all of his critics once and for all. In Game 6, he put up perhaps the greatest power show the Fall Classic has ever seen. In the fourth inning, Jackson blasted the first pitch he saw from LA's Burt Hooton into the right-field stands. One inning later, he faced Elias Sosa. Jackson smacked another homer, again on the first pitch of the at bat.

In the eighth inning, Charlie Hough became Jackson's final victim. The slugger led off the inning, this time pounding Hough's first pitch over the center-field

THE HOME RUN DERBY

Since 1985, many of the league's top sluggers have taken part in an All-Star Game tradition, the Home Run Derby. Although the format has changed over the decades, the basic idea is the same. In a batting-practice setting where pitchers try to serve up easy-to-slug pitches, hitters take turns hitting as many balls over the fence as they can. It's become a highlight of All-Star weekend, often overshadowing the game itself.

The Derby has given fans many memorable performances. In 1991 Cal Ripken Jr.—who was a good, but not spectacular, home-run hitter—thrilled fans with a power surge. In 2008 Josh Hamilton hit 13 homers in a row. And in 2019, Vladimir Guerrero Jr. hit 29 dingers in one round but lost to Pete Alonso (*pictured*) in a classic one-on-one final.

fence. It was Jackson's third home run of the night and his fifth of the series. He powered the Yankees to an 8–4 victory and forever earned the nickname Mr. October.

GIBSON COMES THROUGH
October 15, 1988

Late in Game 1 of the 1988 World Series between the Los Angeles Dodgers and Oakland A's, a television camera scanned the Dodgers dugout. TV commentator Vin Scully mentioned that Dodgers outfielder Kirk Gibson—who was named NL Most Valuable Player (MVP) that year—was nowhere to be found.

Gibson wasn't in the lineup for the Dodgers. He wasn't even in the dugout.

Instead, he was in the clubhouse, getting medical treatment on his injured right leg. Gibson was watching the TV broadcast, and Scully's remark struck him. Gibson could barely walk, but his team needed him. He got off the trainer's table and told manager Tommy Lasorda that he wanted to hit.

The Dodgers were facing a bleak situation. They trailed the A's 4–3 in the bottom of the ninth inning. Oakland closer Dennis Eckersley—one of the most dominant relief pitchers of his era—was on the mound. Eckersley quickly retired the first two batters he faced.

Lasorda knew that the A's weren't expecting the injured Gibson to play. So with the powerful Mike Davis at the plate,

Gibson celebrates as he rounds the bases.

Lasorda sent the light-hitting Dave Anderson to the on-deck circle. It was a trick, and it worked. The A's knew that Davis was dangerous, and they preferred to face Anderson. Eckersley pitched to Davis very carefully, eventually walking him.

Lasorda called Anderson back to the dugout. Gibson hobbled to the plate on his injured leg as the Los Angeles crowd's cheers built to a frenzy.

The game was on the line, and sending the MVP to the plate was no sure thing. Gibson was out of the lineup for a reason. He couldn't run at all, so if he hit anything on the ground, the Dodgers were doomed. Gibson had to hit the ball out of the park, or drive it to an outfield gap and allow Davis to score the tying run. If he hit the ball almost anywhere else, the game was over.

At first, it looked like Lasorda had put too much faith in his injured slugger. Gibson flailed at the first several pitches he saw. "I was just trying to survive," he said. He did survive. Gibson worked Eckersley into a full count.

Eckersley looked in and threw a slider—exactly what Gibson expected. He took a hack. It was an awkward-looking, off-balance swing, but it worked. The ball leaped off Gibson's bat and sailed over the right-field fence. He limped around the bases, pumping his fist, as the crowd went wild.

It was the only plate appearance Gibson had in the 1988 World Series. But it will go down as one of the most magical moments in Dodgers history.

PUCKETT FORCES GAME 7
October 26, 1991

The 1991 World Series between the Minnesota Twins and the Atlanta Braves may have been the greatest ever played. The series was one nail-biter after the next. Of the seven games, five were won by a single run and four were decided on the final play. For pure drama, the 1991 series is hard to top.

Many fans remember the remarkable Game 7, a 1–0 Minnesota victory. The 10-inning win made the Twins world champions. But it was a clutch home run in Game 6 that made that game possible.

The blast came in the 11th inning of a 3–3 tie. Before the game, Twins outfielder Kirby Puckett told his team to climb on his back. He intended to carry them to victory. Puckett had already done his part in the field, robbing Atlanta's Ron Gant of an extra-base hit with a leaping catch in the third inning. But Puckett wasn't done.

The Twins outfielder led off the bottom of the 11th inning for Minnesota. The Braves turned to righty Charlie Leibrandt—a left-handed starter—to pitch in relief. Puckett was lethal against left-handed pitching. Normally a free swinger, he took the first three pitches Leibrandt threw. With the count at two balls and one strike, Leibrandt delivered again. This time, Puckett attacked. He punished the ball, driving it over the wall in left-center field. Puckett's walk-off winner kept the Twins alive and set the stage for the dramatic Game 7.

Joe Carter after his walk-off winner in Game 6

CARTER WALKS OFF
October 23, 1993

A sellout crowd was on hand in Toronto, Canada, for Game 6 of the 1993 World Series. The fans were hoping the hometown Blue Jays could beat the Philadelphia Phillies to clinch the team's second World Series title in a row. They were in for a treat.

The Blue Jays charged out to a 5–1 lead, only to see the Phillies storm back in the seventh to take a 6–5 advantage. That was the score when Toronto came to bat in the bottom of the ninth. Mitch Williams, Philly's lights-out closer, was on the pitcher's mound trying to force Game 7. Williams was nicknamed Wild Thing, and with good reason. He had overpowering pitches—when he could control them. And when he walked the leadoff hitter, Williams gave fans a hint that control could be an issue.

With one out, Paul Molitor smacked a single. The powerful Joe Carter came to the plate with two runners on base. The noise in the stadium was deafening as Carter got ahead in the count, two balls and one strike. Then Williams threw a slider. Carter was fooled by the pitch, and took an ugly swing and miss.

Williams had made Carter look bad on the slider. He could have come back with another one. But instead, he delivered a fastball. This time, Carter was ready. He belted the ball down the left-field line. Carter sprinted toward first base, unsure whether the ball had the distance to clear the fence. It did, tucking just inside the foul pole for a home run. Carter raised his arms in the air as his teammates raced to home plate to greet him. It was the first come-from-behind walk-off winner in World Series history.

"When [Carter] swung and missed at the 2–1 pitch, it didn't look good," Molitor later said. "But the next thing I know is the ball is going out of the ballpark. I wasn't prepared for an ending like that. I had chills."

FREESE BRINGS THE CARDS BACK
October 27, 2011

Not many players in big-league history have had a game quite like David Freese had in the 2011 World Series. Freese and the Cardinals had overcome a 10.5-game deficit in the regular season to earn a place in the playoffs. Then, in the World Series, they trailed the Texas Rangers three games to two. In the bottom of the ninth inning of Game 6, with two outs, the Cards were behind 7–5.

The Cardinals weren't supposed to win. But nobody told Freese. With two runners on, he lined a triple to tie the game. Texas scored in the top of the 10th, and the Cards came back yet again to force an 11th inning.

Texas failed to score in the top of the 11th. Then Freese did his magic again. He led off the inning and worked reliever Mark Lowe to a full count. Lowe

Feeling the tension of an extra-inning game, most Cardinals fans were already on their feet when Freese's home run took flight.

looked in and delivered a changeup. The slow pitch was designed to fool Freese into swinging too quickly. But Freese wasn't fooled. He timed his swing perfectly and crushed the ball. It sailed 429 feet (131 m) over the center-field fence. Freese circled the bases as the St. Louis fans erupted. The Cardinals had once again come back from the brink of elimination. They went on to win Game 7, and Freese was named the series MVP.

4 RECORD BOOK

R uth, Aaron, Mantle, and Jackson. These big swingers and many others are the stuff of legends, and they made their names by crushing the ball over the fence. Learn more about the 25 most prolific home run hitters in MLB history.

NO. 25 MEL OTT

511 home runs
Primary position: outfield
Team: New York Giants
MLB career: 1926–1947
Hall of Fame induction: 1951

Unlike many of the greatest home run hitters, Mel Ott was not a big man. He stood just 5 feet 9 (1.8 m) tall and weighed 170 pounds (77 kg). But he used a quick bat and a great eye at the plate to punish pitchers. The 11-time All Star led the NL in homers six times, and in 1945 he became the first NL player to surpass 500 career home runs.

NO. 23 (TIE) EDDIE MATHEWS

512 home runs
Primary position: third base
Teams: Boston Braves, Milwaukee Braves, Atlanta Braves, Houston Astros, and Detroit Tigers
MLB career: 1952–1968
Hall of Fame induction: 1978

Mathews played for the Braves in three cities. He started his career in 1952 with the Boston Braves. He moved with the team to Milwaukee, Wisconsin, in 1953, and then to Atlanta, Georgia, in 1966. Through it all, the lefty used his powerful swing to become one of the game's most feared hitters. Mathews belted more than 20 homers in each of his first 14 seasons and was named to 12 All-Star teams. After his playing career, he managed the Braves for three years (1972–1974).

Ernie Banks

NO. 23 (TIE) ERNIE BANKS

512 home runs
Primary position: shortstop
Team: Chicago Cubs
MLB career: 1953–1971
Hall of Fame induction: 1977

Mr. Cub, as fans called Ernie Banks, spent his entire MLB career playing for the Cubs. Before that, Banks served in the US Army during the Korean War (1950–1953) and played in the Negro Leagues. Banks hit his peak in 1958 with 47 dingers, and in 1959 he smashed 45 homers, winning back-to-back NL

MVP awards. He remained a highly productive player well into his late 30s, but he never played in the World Series.

NO. 20 (TIE) WILLIE MCCOVEY

521 home runs
Primary position: first base
Teams: San Francisco Giants, San Diego Padres, and Oakland Athletics
MLB career: 1959–1980
Hall of Fame induction: 1986

Nicknamed Stretch because of his long arms and ability to reach almost any ball hit his way, McCovey played in parts of four decades. He burst onto the scene with the Giants in 1959, hitting 13 home runs and winning the Rookie of the Year award. Early on, he wasn't known as a power hitter. But that changed in 1963 when he exploded for 44 dingers. McCovey's best season came in 1969, when he batted .320 with 45 home runs on his way to NL MVP honors.

NO. 20 (TIE) FRANK THOMAS

521 home runs
Primary position: designated hitter
Teams: Chicago White Sox, Oakland Athletics, and Toronto Blue Jays
MLB career: 1990–2008
Hall of Fame induction: 2014

Frank Thomas

The Big Hurt earned his nickname. Frank Thomas stood 6 feet 5 (2 m) tall and put the hurt on AL opponents. Thomas hit for both average and power, with a career batting average of .301. He was the AL MVP in 1993 and 1994. He also won the AL batting title in 1997, hitting .347.

NO. 20 (TIE) TED WILLIAMS

521 home runs
Primary position: outfield
Team: Boston Red Sox
MLB career: 1939–1942, 1946–1960
Hall of Fame induction: 1966

Ted Williams

Many regard Ted Williams as the greatest hitter in baseball history. As he racked up huge home run totals season after season, he kept high batting averages and rarely struck out. Williams was an outstanding contact hitter who just happened to hit the ball out of the park. He batted .406 in 1941, making him the last big-league hitter to hit over .400 in a season. Williams lost three years of his prime while serving in World War II. If he hadn't, he would certainly rank much higher on the all-time home run list.

NO. 19 JIMMIE FOXX

534 home runs
Primary position: first base
Teams: Philadelphia Athletics, Boston Red Sox, Chicago Cubs, and Philadelphia Phillies
MLB career: 1925–1945
Hall of Fame induction: 1951

Babe Ruth paved the way for big-league sluggers, but Jimmie Foxx was right behind him. Foxx hit his 500th home run in 1940 at the age of 32. He remained the youngest to do so until Alex Rodriguez broke the record in 1997. Foxx slugged 30 or more homers in 12 straight seasons from 1929 to 1940. He won three MVP awards and two World Series titles. In 1933 he won the AL Triple Crown by leading the league in home runs, batting average, and RBIs.

NO. 18 MICKEY MANTLE

536 home runs
Primary position: outfield
Team: New York Yankees
MLB career: 1951–1968
Hall of Fame induction: 1974

In the 1950s, Mantle appeared to be on track to challenge Babe Ruth's career home run record. The Mick was perhaps the greatest switch hitter the game has ever seen, with power from both sides of the plate. He was famous for his tape-measure home runs, including his 565-foot (172 m) blast in 1953. Mantle won three AL MVP awards, but injuries derailed his career in the 1960s, leaving him short of the home run record. He retired at the age of 36.

David Ortiz

NO. 17 DAVID ORTIZ

541 home runs
Primary position: designated hitter
Teams: Minnesota Twins and Boston Red Sox
MLB career: 1997–2016
Hall of Fame induction: will be eligible in 2021

Ortiz spent the first six seasons of his career with the Twins. But when he joined the Red Sox in 2003, he burst into stardom. Boston fans knew Big Papi for his clutch hitting. In 2004 he helped the Red Sox win the World Series for the first time since 1918. His best season may have been 2006, when he hit a career-high 54 dingers. He retired in 2016, still at the top of his game. At the age of 40, Ortiz batted .315 and hit 38 home runs in his final campaign. Many consider him a shoo-in to join the Hall of Fame.

NO. 16 MIKE SCHMIDT

548 home runs
Primary position: third base
Team: Philadelphia Phillies
MLB career: 1972–1989
Hall of Fame induction: 1995

Many fans, players, and managers call Mike Schmidt the greatest third baseman of all time. He was a wizard in the field, winning 10 Gold Glove Awards as the best fielder at his position. And he was a terror at the plate. Schmidt was the NL MVP three times (1980, 1981, and 1986) and led the NL in homers eight times. He is also one of only a handful of players to have hit four homers in a single game.

NO. 15 MANNY RAMIREZ

555 home runs
Primary position: outfield
Teams: Cleveland Indians, Boston Red Sox, Los Angeles Dodgers, Chicago White Sox, and Tampa Bay Rays
MLB career: 1993–2011
Hall of Fame induction: eligible since 2017

Manny Ramirez

Manny Ramirez may have been the greatest right-handed hitter of his era. His smooth, strong stroke led to a career .312 batting average and 555 home runs. Ramirez was at his best in the clutch. His 29 postseason homers are the most in MLB history, while his 21 career grand slams rank third all time. Ramirez retired in 2011 when he faced a 100-game suspension for taking PEDs. It's unclear how Ramirez's steroid use will affect his future Hall of Fame status.

NO. 14 REGGIE JACKSON

563 home runs
Primary position: outfield
Teams: Oakland Athletics, Baltimore Orioles, New York Yankees, and California Angels
MLB career: 1967–1987
Hall of Fame induction: 1993

Mr. October was a big-time clutch player. Jackson was part of five World Series winners—three with the A's and two with the Yankees—and hit 18 postseason long balls. Jackson's finest season may have been 1973. He batted .293 and hit 32 homers on his way to winning the AL MVP award.

NO. 13 RAFAEL PALMEIRO

569 home runs
Primary position: first base
Teams: Chicago Cubs, Texas Rangers, and Baltimore Orioles
MLB career: 1986–2005
Hall of Fame induction: eligible since 2011

Rafael Palmeiro was all about consistency. He never led the league in home runs, and he never finished higher than fifth in MVP voting. What he did was collect home runs season after season. The left-handed slugger topped 30 homers 10 times. He is one of only six big leaguers to join the 500-home-run club and the 3,000-hit club. Allegations of steroid use that followed Palmeiro for much of his career are the likely reason he has not been inducted into the Hall of Fame.

NO. 12 HARMON KILLEBREW

573 home runs
Primary position: first base
Teams: Washington Senators, Minnesota Twins, and Kansas City Royals
MLB career: 1954–1975
Hall of Fame induction: 1984

Harmon Killebrew debuted with the Washington Senators in 1954. But for his first five seasons, he barely played. Finally, in 1959, he got his chance. He made it count, belting a league-leading 42 home runs. Killebrew terrorized American League pitching for the next decade and a half, most of it with the Twins. The 1969 AL MVP was known for his quick swing and ultra-long homers.

NO. 11 MARK MCGWIRE

583 home runs
Primary position: first base
Teams: Oakland Athletics and St. Louis Cardinals
MLB career: 1986–2001
Hall of Fame induction: was on the ballot from 2007 to 2016 but didn't get enough votes

Big Mac burst onto the baseball scene with the A's in 1987. The 23-year-old smashed 49 home runs and won Rookie of the Year. It was just the beginning. McGwire was the premier power hitter of the 1990s. In 1998 he hit 70 round-trippers and shattered Roger Maris's single-season home run record. McGwire later admitted to using steroids during much of his career. For that reason, he has not been voted into the Hall of Fame.

NO. 10 FRANK ROBINSON

586 home runs
Primary position: outfield
Teams: Cincinnati Reds, Baltimore Orioles, Los Angeles Dodgers, California Angels, and Cleveland Indians
MLB career: 1956–1976
Hall of Fame induction: 1982

Frank Robinson debuted with the Reds at the age of 20, and he made an instant impact. He blasted 38 round-trippers and won the NL Rookie of the Year award. It was the start of an amazing run. Robinson hit 15 or more homers for 19 straight seasons from 1956 to 1974. He won MVP awards in both leagues and made 14 All-Star teams. Robinson went on to a long and successful career as a manager after his playing days ended.

NO. 9 SAMMY SOSA

609 home runs
Primary position: outfield
Teams: Texas Rangers, Chicago White Sox, Chicago Cubs, and Baltimore Orioles
MLB career: 1989–2005, 2007
Hall of Fame induction: eligible since 2013

Slammin' Sammy started his career with the Rangers and White Sox. But it wasn't until he joined the Cubs that he became one of the game's most feared hitters. Sosa was a free swinger who often took an all-or-nothing approach at the plate. He piled up home runs as well as strikeouts. In 1998 he lost the home run chase to Mark McGwire, but Sosa won the NL MVP award. Steroid accusations haunted Sosa during his career with the Cubs, and he has not been inducted into the Hall of Fame.

NO. 8 JIM THOME

612 home runs
Primary position: first base
Teams: Cleveland Indians, Philadelphia Phillies, Chicago White Sox, Los Angeles Dodgers, Minnesota Twins, and Baltimore Orioles
MLB career: 1991–2012

Jim Thome

Hall of Fame induction: 2018

Standing 6 feet 4 (1.9 m) and weighing 250 pounds (113 kg), Jim Thome was a fearsome figure at the plate. He used pure strength to muscle the ball out of the park. Late in his career, Thome played mostly as a designated hitter. He bounced from team to team and succeeded almost everywhere he went. In 2011 with the Twins, he became just the eighth player to join the 600-homer club.

NO. 7 KEN GRIFFEY JR.

630 home runs
Primary position: outfield
Teams: Seattle Mariners, Cincinnati Reds, and Chicago White Sox
MLB career: 1989–2010
Hall of Fame induction: 2016

Ken Griffey Jr.

The Kid came into the big leagues at the age of 19 as one of the most exciting young players in history. Griffey's father, Ken Griffey Sr., had been a star with the Reds. With a smooth stroke, pure speed, and fantastic defense, the younger Griffey had all the tools to be a star. His finest season came in 1997. He batted .304 and hit 56 home runs, earning AL MVP honors. Injuries slowed Griffey late in his career, robbing him of a chance to chase down the all-time career home run record.

NO. 6 WILLIE MAYS

660 home runs
Primary position: outfield
Teams: San Francisco Giants and New York Mets
MLB career: 1951–1952, 1954–1973
Hall of Fame induction: 1979

Willie Mays

Willie Mays was one of MLB's biggest superstars after the league began to integrate in 1947. He started his career in the Negro Leagues before setting the National League on fire with the Giants. He won the NL MVP in 1954 and again in 1965. He was a speedster, a brilliant fielder, and an ultra-powerful hitter. Nicknamed the Say Hey Kid, many experts call him the greatest baseball player of all time.

NO. 5 ALBERT PUJOLS

662 home runs
Primary position: first base
Teams: St. Louis Cardinals and Los Angeles Angels
MLB career: 2001–present
Hall of Fame induction: eligible five years after retirement

The only active player on the top-25 career home run list, Pujols has been one of the game's best hitters since he debuted with the Cardinals at the age of 21. A three-time MVP (2005, 2008, and 2009), Pujols possesses the rare ability to hit for power with a high batting average. His finest years came in St. Louis. His numbers have dipped since signing with the Angels in 2012, but he continues to climb the list with season after season of big home run totals.

NO. 4 ALEX RODRIGUEZ

696 home runs
Primary position: shortstop
Teams: Seattle Mariners, Texas Rangers, and New York Yankees
MLB career: 1994–2013, 2015–2016
Hall of Fame induction: eligible in 2022

A-Rod set a new standard for power from a middle infielder. He hit for average and power and played reliable defense in the field. The three-time MVP (2003, 2005, and 2007) also played third base and designated hitter later in his career. Many call Rodriguez the greatest player of his generation. An admission of steroid use tarnished his legacy, however.

NO. 3 BABE RUTH

714 home runs
Primary position: outfield
Teams: Boston Red Sox, New York Yankees, and Boston Braves
MLB career: 1914–1935
Hall of Fame induction: 1936

No player in history changed the game as Babe Ruth did. The Bambino started out as an outstanding pitcher before becoming the first great home run hitter. In 1918 he led the AL with 11 home runs. In 1919 he upped his total to 29. Then, in 1920, he hit 54 long balls! Ruth was the anchor of a powerful Yankees lineup that fans called Murderers' Row. He launched the Yankees dynasty and remains the standard for what a great power hitter can be.

NO. 2 HANK AARON

755 home runs
Primary position: outfield
Teams: Milwaukee Braves, Atlanta Braves, and Milwaukee Brewers
MLB career: 1954–1976
Hall of Fame induction: 1982

Hammerin' Hank stands second on the all-time home run list, but because of the steroids era, many still regard him as the true long-ball king. Aaron was reliable and consistent. He batted .300 or better 14 times and hit 30 or more homers 15 times. He appeared in 25 All-Star Games, won the 1957 NL MVP award, and led the Milwaukee Braves to a World Series title in 1957. His 2,297 RBIs remain the most in MLB history.

NO. 1 BARRY BONDS

762 home runs
Primary position: outfield
Teams: Pittsburgh Pirates and San Francisco Giants
MLB career: 1986–2007
Hall of Fame induction: eligible since 2013

Barry Bonds

Barry Bonds was destined for greatness. His godfather was Willie Mays. Bonds's father, Bobby, was a star outfielder for the Giants. Barry Bonds had it all: speed, power, and a nearly perfect eye at the plate. The seven-time MVP holds the records for most home runs in a season (73) and the most career walks (2,558). Bonds has not been inducted into the Hall of Fame, however, because of allegations of steroid use.

5 THE FUTURE OF THE LONG BALL

What is the future for baseball and the home run? The steroids era has passed, yet players continue to hit long balls at record paces. How can MLB slow down the rate of home runs—and does it even want to?

People have different opinions about the role of home runs in MLB. Homers are exciting, and some fans argue that baseball needs more dingers to compete with the popularity of action-packed sports such as football and basketball. Others argue that the home run surge takes away from long-standing traditions of the game. Teams used to manufacture runs by getting runners on base and moving them around the bases with singles and bunts. In the modern game, most teams try to hit home runs every at bat, even when they have runners on base. Critics think this lack of variety drives away fans.

Max Scherzer gave up 18 home runs to opposing hitters in 2019, one of the lowest totals of his career.

If MLB wants to decrease home run totals, many players argue that the first step is to examine how baseballs are made. MLB insists that the physical characteristics of baseballs haven't changed in the modern live ball era. But some players don't believe it. "Yes, the ball is different," said Washington Nationals pitcher Max Scherzer. "We see lower and lower exit [velocities] that are going for home runs. That's why players want answers." Scherzer and others think baseballs in the live ball era produce less drag in the air, allowing them to fly farther.

Other options to lower home run rates include moving back outfield fences and raising pitcher's mounds. With fences placed farther from home plate, fewer balls would clear them. A higher mound would allow pitchers to throw downhill, getting more velocity and downward movement on balls.

Yet while some fans and players object to the increased rate of home runs and the changes it has brought to the game, others love it. Home runs get crowds on their feet. Big blasts make up the majority of baseball highlight videos. They generate excitement that no other play in the sport can match. For more than a century, the home run has been the identity of Major League Baseball. It will probably remain king for another century to come.

Most fans love the aggressive at bats and flashy styles of young baseball superstars such as Fernando Tatis Jr.

HOME RUN RECORDS

All stats are through the 2020 MLB season.

Most Season Home Runs by a Player

1. Barry Bonds (2001) 73
2. Mark McGwire (1998) 70
3. Sammy Sosa (1998) 66
4. Mark McGwire (1999) 65
5. Sammy Sosa (2001) 64
6. Sammy Sosa (1999) 63
7. Roger Maris (1961) 61
8. Babe Ruth (1927) 60
9. Babe Ruth (1921) 59
   Giancarlo Stanton (2017) 59

Most Season Home Runs by a Team

1. Minnesota Twins (2019) 307
2. New York Yankees (2019) 306
3. Houston Astros (2019) 288
4. Los Angeles Dodgers (2019) 279
5. New York Yankees (2018) 267
6. Seattle Mariners (1997) 264
7. Texas Rangers (2005) 260
8. Oakland Athletics (2019) 257
   Toronto Blue Jays (2010) 257
   Baltimore Orioles (1996) 257

Most Home Runs by a Rookie

1. Pete Alonso (2019) 53
2. Aaron Judge (2017) 52
3. Mark McGwire (1987) 49
4. Cody Bellinger (2017) 39
5. Wally Berger (1930) 38
   Frank Robinson (1956) 38
7. Albert Pujols (2001) 37
   Al Rosen (1950) 37
9. Jose Abreu (36) 2014
10. Mike Piazza (1993) 35
    Ron Kittle (1983) 35
    Rudy York (1937) 35
    Hal Trosky (1934) 35

Most Career Grand Slams

1. Alex Rodriguez 25
2. Lou Gehrig 23
3. Manny Ramirez 21
4. Eddie Murray 19
5. Willie McCovey 18
   Robin Ventura 18
7. Jimmie Foxx 17
   Carlos Lee 17
   Ted Williams 17
10. Hank Aaron 16
    Dave Kingman 16
    Babe Ruth 16

Most Career Home Runs Allowed by a Pitcher

1. Jamie Moyer 522
2. Robin Roberts 505
3. Fergie Jenkins 484
4. Phil Niekro 482
5. Don Sutton 472
6. Frank Tanana 448
7. Bartolo Colon 439
8. Warren Spahn 434
9. Bert Blyleven 430
10. Tim Wakefield 418

Most Games in a Row with a Home Run

1. Ken Griffey Jr (1993) 8
   Don Mattingly (1987) 8
   Dale Long (1956) 8
4. Kendrys Morales (2018) 7
   Kevin Mench (2006) 7
   Barry Bonds (2004) 7
   Jim Thome (2002) 7

Players Who Hit Four Home Runs in a Game

Lou Gehrig (1932)
Chuck Klein (1936)
Pat Seerey (1948)
Gil Hodges (1950)
Joe Adcock (1954)
Rocky Colavito (1959)
Willie Mays (1961)
Mike Schmidt (1976)
Bob Horner (1986)
Mark Whiten (1993)
Mike Cameron (2002)
Shawn Green (2002)
Carlos Delgado (2003)
Josh Hamilton (2012)
Scooter Gennett (2017)
J. D. Martinez (2017)

GLOSSARY

anabolic steroids: drugs that promote muscle growth and are sometimes abused by athletes

changeup: a slow pitch in baseball thrown with the same motion as a fastball so as to deceive the batter

clutch: a high-pressure situation, often late in a game or in the playoffs

commissioner: the executive in charge of a sports league

earned run average (ERA): the average number of earned runs a pitcher gives up per nine innings

elevation: a measure of how far something is above sea level

exit velocity: the speed at which the ball leaves the bat

full count: when the count to the batter is three balls and two strikes

kinetic energy: the energy of motion

launch angle: the angle at which the ball leaves the bat

line drive: a batted ball hit in a nearly straight line usually not far above the ground

RBI: a run in baseball that is driven in by a batter

slider: a breaking pitch that is faster than a curveball but with less movement

upset: an unexpected defeat

walk-off: ending a baseball game by causing the winning run to score for the home team in the bottom of the last inning

SOURCE NOTES

14 Bill Plaschke, "Baseball Should Come Clean for Roger Maris," *Los Angeles Times*, October 11, 2011, https://www.latimes.com/archives/la-xpm-2011-oct-01-la-sp-1002-plaschke-roger-maris-20111002-story .html.

24 "How Far Can You Hit One?," Science of Baseball, accessed June 1, 2020, https://www.exploratorium .edu/baseball/features/how-far-can-you-hit-one.html.

29–30 Nick Anapolis, "Mantle Hits 565-Foot Home Run," National Baseball Hall of Fame," accessed June 1, 2020, https://baseballhall.org/discover/inside-pitch/mantle-hits-565-foot-home-run.

32 Bob Nightengale, "Despite Hate Mail, Threats, Hank Aaron 'Was Never Scared.' Behind the Scenes When Aaron Broke Babe Ruth's HR Record," *USA Today*, April 8, 2020, https://www.usatoday.com/story /sports/mlb/columnist/bob-nightengale/2020/04/08/hank-aaron-breaks-babe-ruth-home-run-record -anniversary/2959949001/.

37 Mike Lopresti, "Kirk Gibson's 1988 Home Run Still a World Series Highlight," *USA Today*, accessed June 1, 2020, https://usatoday30.usatoday.com/sports/baseball/playoffs/2008-10-06-gibson-88homer_N.htm.

39 Rick Weinberg, "43: Joe Carter's Home Runs Wins 1993 World Series," ESPN, July 26, 2004, https:// www.espn.com/espn/espn25/story?page=moments/43.

56 Barry Svrluga, "Home Runs Are Slowly Killing Baseball, and Something Needs to Be Done," *Washington Post*, July 9, 2019, https://www.washingtonpost.com/sports/home-runs-are-slowly-killing-baseball-and -something-needs-to-be-done/2019/07/09/c0d42e06-a271-11e9-b732-41a79c2551bf_story.html.

FURTHER READING

Books

DeMocker, Michael. *Babe Ruth and Lou Gehrig*. Kennett Square, PA: Purple Toad, 2020.

Doeden, Matt. *The Negro Leagues: Celebrating Baseball's Unsung Heroes*. Minneapolis: Millbrook Press, 2017.

Lyons, Douglas B. *The New York Yankees Home Run Almanac: The Bronx Bombers' Most Historic, Unusual, and Titanic Dingers*. New York: Sports, 2018.

Websites

Baseball Reference
https://www.baseball-reference.com/

ESPN.com: MLB
https://www.espn.com/mlb/

National Baseball Hall of Fame
https://baseballhall.org/

Negro Leagues Baseball Museum
https://nlbm.com/

The Official Site of Major League Baseball
https://www.mlb.com/

INDEX

ABOUT THE AUTHOR

Matt Doeden began his career as a sportswriter, covering everything from high school sports to the NFL. Since then he has written hundreds of children's and young adult books on topics ranging from history to sports to current events. His book *Darkness Everywhere: The Assassination of Mohandas Gandhi* was listed among the Best Children's Books of the Year by the Children's Book Committee at Bank Street College. Doeden lives in Minnesota with his wife and two children.

Photo Acknowledgments

Image credits: Dan Thornberg/ Shutterstock.com; Vector Tradition/Shutterstock.com (design elements). AP Photo/John Cordes/Icon Sportswire, p. 4; AP Photo/Brian Rothmuller/Icon Sportswire, p. 6; Chicago Sun-Times/Chicago Daily News collection/Chicago History Museum/Getty Images, p. 8; AP Photo, pp. 9, 10, 12, 14, 15 (top), 29, 44, 52, Wikimedia Commons (Public Domain), p. 11; AP Photo/William J. Smith, p. 13; Icon and Image/Getty Images, p. 15 (bottom); AP Photo/Mary Butkus, p. 16; Laura Westlund/Independent Picture Service, pp. 20-21; AP Photo/Frank Franklin II, p. 22 (top); AP Photo/ Kyodo Extra, pp. 22 (bottom), 35; AP Photo/Rick Ulreich/Icon Sportswire, p. 24; AP Photo/Dustin Bradford, p. 25; B. Bennett/Getty Images, p. 27; AP Photo/Harry Harris, p. 31; Bettmann/Getty Images, p. 33; AP Photo/Ray Stubblebine, p. 34; AP Photo/Rusty Kennedy, p. 36; AP Photo/Hans Deryk, p. 38; AP Photo/Charlie Riedel, p. 40; AP Photo/David Durochik, p. 42; AP Photo/Cliff Welch/Icon Sportswire, p. 43; AP Photo/Michael Dwyer, p. 46; AP Photo/Tony Dejak, p. 47; AP Photo/Mark Duncan, p. 50; AP Photo/David Durochik, p. 51; AP Photo/Jeff Chiu, p. 54; AP Photo/Nick Wass, p. 56; AP Photo/Gregory Bull, p. 57.

Cover: Dustin Bradford/Icon Sportswire/Getty Images; Bettmann/Getty Images; Vector Tradition/Shutterstock.com.